Directors' Guide

for the
Preparation Days
Retreat

Director's Guide

For the Preparation Days Retreat

Five Weeks of Ignatian Prayer

By Ellen Tomaszewski

Director's Guide
Preparation Days Retreat

By Ellen Tomaszewski

Published by **Etcetera Press LLC**
Richland, WA

& etcetera press

Copyright © 2013 by Ellen Tomaszewski

All rights reserved. No part of this book may be reproduced, stored in a retrieval system, or transmitted in any form or by any means, electronic, mechanical, photocopying, or otherwise, without written permission of Ellen Tomaszewski or Etcetera Press LLC.

Table of Contents

Group Spiritual Direction Instructions 11
Opening Prayer 12
Closing Prayer 13

Meeting 1 14
Meeting 2 18
Meeting 3 21
Meeting 4 24
Meeting 5 27

Apendix
Sample Presentations

1 - Beginning to Pray 32
2 - The Life of Ignatius of Loyola 37
3 - Guided Meditation 43
4 - Principle and Foundation 45
5 - Choosing the Exercises 50

Sample Brochure 54

Meeting Schedule Overview 59

Welcome to the Preparation Days Retreat

This retreat is set up for anyone who wants to learn to pray the Ignatian way. It can be used as a prelude to the full Spiritual Exercises, 19th annotation, or it can stand alone.

All the materials are provided. For each participant you will need a Preparation Days Retreat Participant Booklet.

Also, each participant should have a Preparation Days Retreat Faith Autobiography Booklet. This will be handed in as part of the application for those who continue into the full Spiritual Exercises.

Each director needs a copy of the Preparation Days Retreat Director Handbook for their use.

Director's Guide

About the Preparation Days Retreat

This Preparation Days Retreat is a five-week introduction into the Spiritual Exercises of St. Ignatius. Retreatants participate in group spiritual direction and hear about certain aspects of the Exercises, including how to begin to pray, the Principle and Foundation, and the life of St. Ignatius. And they are given an opportunity to practice Ignatian contemplation and meditation. The five-week venue allows participants to try Ignatian Spirituality without a full year commitment.

For groups using this retreat as a springboard for the full 19th annotation of the Exercises, the Preparation Days Retreat provides a way in which directors and retreatants get to know each other before they are matched up. Because of the weekly meetings, directors have a better idea of who is ready to make the Exercises.

Moving into individual spiritual direction after group spiritual direction
The Preparation Days experience seemed to facilitate future direction. If your group provides the Spiritual Exercises in Everyday Life (19th Annotation), your meeting after this retreat would be on the First Week material (sin and sinfulness). Participants who have experienced the Preparation Days Retreat are ready to move into the First Week material of the Spiritual Exercises.

Matching directors with directees
For groups that continue on into the full 19th Annotation of the Spiritual Exercises, matching directors with directees can be done as usual. Prayerful reflection over faith autobiographies and time availability are the main concerns in matching directors to directees. For more on providing the Spiritual Exercises with groups, see *Taking the Exercises to the World* by Ellen Tomaszewski.

Individual direction vs. group direction during Prep Days
The group process builds community in unexpected ways. People get to know each other and feel more comfortable with members of the group and the retreat directors through this process. Also, they are exposed to group spiritual direction. Of course, the choice is yours.

Continuing on to the 19th Annotation of the Spiritual Exercises
About half of our participants continue into the Exercises from the Preparation Days Retreat. Your results may differ. But in general, our numbers of participants increased when we began with the Preparation Days Retreat.

Director's Guide

General Instructions to Begin

- Collect your group leaders. (You'll need about one for every four participants.)
- Order one Preparation Days Retreat Director Guide for each director.
- Arrange a place and time and fee, if any.
- Advertise in church bulletins, community event listings, newspapers (if possible) and word of mouth. Give pulpit talks.
- Collect name, address, phone, e-mail, and fee of participants.
- Order one Participant Booklet and Faith Autobiography Booklet for each participant.
- Call or e-mail participants the week before the event to welcome them to the program and remind them of the meeting.
- Meet with all group leaders at least two weeks before the first meeting.
    - Fill out the schedule, arranging who does what job on the actual retreat days.
    - If your group members are unfamiliar with group spiritual direction, review and practice group supervision following the rules in this Director Guide, below.
    - Choose one person to create a prayerful environment for the retreat days.

Group Spiritual Direction Instructions

The purpose of Group Spiritual Direction is to keep our focus on what God is doing.

- No problem solving.
- No advice giving.
- Keep the focus on the person who is sharing.

Each person in the group is invited to share their reflection. Any participant does not have to share if he or she doesn't not want to, but, keep in mind this is how group spiritual direction works. Sharing gives The Spirit an opportunity to be active within the group process.

- How did this reading affect you as you prayed?
- Share your experience.
- Share a feeling.
- Where was God in this experience?

When a person is speaking, listeners are asked to focus on the one speaking. Listen for God in what the person is sharing. What is God saying to that person? What is God saying to you as you listen?

After a person has shared, the facilitator will invite you all to share your response to what you have *heard*.

- Share what you feel God is saying to that person.

- Share what you feel God is saying to you.

Director's Guide

Opening Prayer

Use this prayer for each meeting.

1st Reader:
Jesus said, "Where two or three people come together in my name, I am there with you." Lord Jesus, here we are, gathered together in your name. So we ask you to help us see you today in this meeting.

2nd Reader:
Jesus, you told us, "I am the light of the world… Whoever follows me will have the light of life and will never walk in darkness." (John 8:12)
We ask that you let the light of this candle symbolize your presence here among us, right now.

If permitted to do so in your facility, light the candle.

3rd Reader:
Lord Jesus, we believe that wherever you are, the Father and Holy Spirit are there, too. So we begin our meeting in your presence and the name of the Father, the Son, and the Holy Spirit.

Amen.

Closing Prayer

Use this prayer to close each meeting.

1st Reader:
As we end our meeting, let's listen to the words Simeon spoke to Mary and Joseph in the temple about their child, Jesus.

2nd Reader:
"Now Master...my eyes have seen the salvation which you have prepared for all the nations to see, a light to enlighten the pagans and the glory of your people Israel." (Luke 2: 30-32)
Glory be to the Father, the Son, and the Holy Spirit.
Blow out the candle.

3rd Reader:
Lord, thank-you for your salvation, which enlightens the whole world. We know that even though we've blown out our candle, Christ's light continues to burn through and in each of us. Help us this week to let that light shine to others.

Now, together, let's pray the Lord's Prayer: "Our Father…"

Amen.

Director's Guide

Meeting 1

Date: _____

Purpose of Meeting
- Introduce participants to each other
- Introduce participants to prayer methods and helps
- Begin faith autobiographies

Agenda

Min	Activity	Who
30	Introductions, Welcome, Icebreaker	
5	Opening prayer with ritual (p. 12)	
20	Talk on Method of Prayer (See Appendix for example)	
5	Silent meditation on questions provided in booklet	
10	Break	
35	Small Group Spiritual Direction – Answer why am I here and what do I hope to gain? (p. 11)	
10	Q&A – large group discussion and feedback	
3	Preparation for next meeting - hand out booklets for daily prayer and faith autobiography workbook	
2	Closing Prayer (p. 13)	
Environment: candle, picture or statue of Christ, cloth, small table			

Icebreaker Activity

Pair participants together in twos. Allow 3-4 min. for one person to interview the other, then switch.

Go around the room. Let each person of the pair introduce the other to the group.

OR:

Go around the circle letting each person introduce him- or herself.
- Each person says his or her first name and the reason (one or two words only) why he/she came to the retreat.
- The next person must say each previous name along with each person's reason for coming.
- When the discussion goes all around the circle and returns to the facilitator, he/she lists the name of every participant and the reason they came.

Or: create your own ice breaker activity. Make it fun and memorable.

Opening Prayer - (page 12)

Divide the group into small groups

Keep the same groups throughout this retreat. Tell participants what room or area they'll be meeting in. Introduce the group guide. Explain how the groups will work. To make the meeting run smoother, you can plan ahead who will be in which group.

My Group consists of these people:

1._____

2._____

3. _____

4. _____

Director's Guide

Talk on Method for Prayer (See Appendix)

Silent Meditation

Give participants time to pray on their own. Decide whether they can go to different parts of the room or building, or outside if the weather permits. Set a time for them to return and announce it. You can have a bell or other method to call them back if they disburse.

Questions for Silent Meditation

- Where have I found God in the last week or so?
- Why am I here and what do I hope to gain?
- What, if anything, am I afraid of when I consider God or this retreat?

Please write thoughts and feelings about your prayer here.

_____

_____

_____

_____

_____

_____

_____

_____

_____

_____

_____

_____

_____

_____

Break

Small Group Spiritual Direction
- Review rules for sharing in the small groups.
- Send participants to small groups.
- Follow group spiritual direction instructions (page 11).

Large Group Question and Answer Session
Give members of the group time to discuss anything they think is important that came up during the small group sharing and answer any questions.

Instructions for the Coming Week
Tell participants:
- How to use their books this coming week
- About the Faith Autobiography Workbook.
- Show them how to find each days's question
- To fill in pages of both booklets daily
- Date and time for next meeting

Closing Prayer - (page 13)

Director's Guide

Meeting 2

Date _____

Purposes of Meeting
- Introduce Ignatius
- Practice group spiritual direction

Agenda

Min	Activity	Who
5	Introductions, Welcome	
5	Opening prayer with ritual – page 12	
10	Feedback – questions about previous meeting, prayer experiences, etc.	
20	Presentation on Ignatius' life from the view of his aunt, Madalena (see Appendix for example.)	
10	Silent meditation on questions provided	
10	Break	
5	Review Group Spiritual Direction instructions - page 11	
45	Group spiritual direction (with your assigned group)	
5	Instructions for following week prayer	
5	Closing prayer – page 13	
Environment – Picture of Ignatius, Montserrat, cloth, candle, potted plant, low table or box.		

Introduction and Welcome

Opening Prayer (page 12)

Feedback

Allow members of the group to ask questions or comment on the previous meeting, prayer experiences, writing in their journal, the Faith Autobiography, or whatever else they want to discus.

Silent Meditation - Questions

- What attracts, repels, or surprises me about Ignatius' life?
- How does hearing about Ignatius affect me?
- How am I feeling at this moment about this retreat?
- What has God been telling me this past week? Is there a general theme that I can sort out or not?

Director's Guide

_____

_____

_____

Break

Small Group Spiritual Direction

- Review rules for sharing in the small groups.
- Send participants to small groups.
- Follow group spiritual direction instructions (page 11)

Large Group Question and Answer Session

Give members of the group time to discuss anything they think is important that came up during the small group sharing and answer any questions.

Instructions for the Coming Week

Tell participants:
- Review how to pray (brief summary)
- The importance of journaling
- Remind about the Faith Autobiography Workbook
- Announce the date and time for next meeting

Closing Prayer (page 13)

Meeting 3

Date _____

Purposes of Meeting
- Introduce meditation by walking group through one
- Practice group spiritual direction

Before the meeting begins, set the environment. See below for ideas and items you can use. Can be the same for each meeting.

Min.	Activity	Who
5	Introductions, Welcome	
5	Opening prayer with ritual (page 12)	
10	Feedback – questions about previous meeting, prayer experiences, etc	
20	Guided Meditation (see Appendix)	
10	Silent individual meditation on questions provided in participant booklet and below	
10	Break	
5	Review Group Spiritul Direction instructions (page 11)	
45	Group spiritual direction - 3-5 people	
5	Instructions for following week's prayer	
5	Closing prayer (page 13)	
Environment - low table, candle, cloth, flowers, picture of Jesus or icon, weaving.		

Director's Guide

Introduction and Welcome

Opening Prayer (page 12)

Guided Meditation (See Appendix)

Feedback

Allow members of the group to ask questions or comment on the previous meeting, prayer experiences, writing in their journal, the Faith Autobiography, or whatever else they want to discus.

Silent Meditation Questions

- What did you experience when you realized Jesus was speaking to you?
- How did you feel seeing the people who love you?
- What story that you told Jesus touched you the most and why?

_____

_____

_____

_____

Break

Small Group Spiritual Direction
- Review rules for sharing in the small groups.
- Send participants to small groups.
- Follow group spiritual direction instructions (page 11).

Large Group Q & A
Give members of the group time to discuss anything they think is important that came up during the small group sharing and answer any questions.

Instructions for the Coming Week
- Review how to pray (brief summary)
- The importance of journaling
- Remind about the Faith Autobiography Workbook
- Announce the date and time for next meeting
- Add any announcements for your group

Closing Prayer
(page 13)

Director's Guide

Meeting 4

Date _____

Purposes of meeting
- Practice group spiritual direction
- Teach the Principle and Foundation
- Practice silent meditation

Before the meeting begins, set the environment.

Min.	Activity	Who
5	Introductions, Welcome	
5	Opening prayer ritual (p. 12)	
10	Feedback – questions about previous meeting, prayer experiences, etc	
20	Talk on the Principle & Foundation	
10	Silent meditation on questions	
10	Break	
5	Review Group Spiritual Direction instructions	
45	Small group spiritual direction in assigned groups	
5	Instructions for following week's prayer	
5	Closing prayer (page 13)	
Environment - low table, candle, cloth, flowers, picture of Jesus or icon, weaving, poster, open Bible		

Introduction and Welcome

Opening Prayer (page 12)

Feedback

Allow members of the group to ask questions or comment on the previous meeting, prayer experiences, writing in their journal, the Faith Autobiography, or whatever else they want to discus.

Silent Meditation Questions
- How does my current spiritual foundation compare to the one Ignatius proposed in his Principle and Foundation?
- Do I feel that my spiritual foundation is adequate? Why or why not? What would make it better?
- Name some of the values that I hold that influence my choices.

Director's Guide

_____

_____

_____

_____

_____

Break

Small Group Spiritual Direction

- Review rules for sharing in the small groups.
- Send participants to small groups.
- Follow group spiritual direction instructions (page 11)

Large Group Q & A

Give members of the group time to discuss anything they think is important that came up during the small group sharing and answer any questions.

Instructions for the Coming Week

Tell participants:
- Review how to pray (brief summary)
- The importance of journaling
- Remind about the Faith Autobiography Workbook
- Announce the date and time for next meeting
- Add any announcements for your group

Closing Prayer

(Page 13)

Meeting 5

Date _____

Purposes of meeting
- Practice group spiritual direction
- Collect completed faith autobiographies of those continuing into the Exercises
- Explain the Spiritual Exercises and what comes next (if you'll be providing them.)

Before the meeting begins, set the environment.

Min	Activity	Who
5	Introductions, Welcome	
5	Opening prayer with ritual (p. 12)	
10	Feedback – questions about last meeting, prayer experiences, etc.	
15	Talk on choosing the Exercises	
10	Silent meditation questions provided	
10	Break	
2	Review Group Spiritual Direction instructions (p. 11)	
40	Small group spiritual direction	
10	Large group discussion on Exercises.	
2	Collect faith autobiographies and applications of those who wish to continue	
9	Evaluation	
2	Closing prayer (p. 13)	
Environment - low table, candle, cloth, flowers, picture of Jesus or icon, weaving, Bible, exercise equipment			

Introduction and Welcome

Opening Prayer (page 12)

Feedback

Allow members of the group to ask questions or comment on the previous meeting, prayer experiences, writing in their journal, the Faith Autobiography, or whatever else they want to discus.

Talk on Continuing into the Exercises

Silent Meditation

Meditation Questions

- What gifts have I received from the Preparation Days Retreat?
- What are some of the misgivings I have about committing to the Retreat?
- Which of those are from God? Which are from myself?
- Where do I believe God is calling me right now?

Break

Small Group Spiritual Direction
- Review rules for sharing in the small groups.
- Send participants to small groups.
- Follow group spiritual direction instructions (page 11).

Large Group Discussion – Continuing on into the Exercises
Call all groups back together. Let participants discuss what it means to them to continue into the full Spiritual Exercises, (if that's an option).

Collect Faith Autobiographies
For those continuing into the full Spiritul Exercises, you'll need their faith authobiography workbooks to help assign director to directee. Collect these now from those continuing on with the program.

Evaluation
Provide an opportunity for participants to comment on the retreat experience. Ask these questions, or give them time to write answers to these questions:
- What did you like about this retreat?
- Were there any difficult or confusing parts? If so, what were they and how could we have made them better?
- What worked for you? What didn't? Why?

Announcements
Review how to pray (brief summary)
The importance of journaling
Announce the date and time for next meeting

Closing Prayer (p. 13)

Appendix

Handout - One Method for Prayer (5 P's & C)
Also in the Participant Booklet

Place

Remember that God prays in us. So stop and let it happen. Of course, it helps when listening to God to have a quiet, sacred space where you will be undisturbed. Choose a place where you can relax and be uninhibited in your response to God. Use the same place daily.

Passage

Mark your Bible the day before with the scripture so that it will be ready the next day when you pray. You may also find it helpful to read the passage through a day ahead. This allows the scripture to unfold, giving your subconscious time to explore it.

Posture

Practice quiet of body and spirit. Before you read scripture or pray, relax your body. Don't rush. If this takes up the whole prayer time, that's okay. Quiet your mind. Breathe deeply and listen to sounds (or quiet) around you. Then sink into the silence of your sacred space.

Presence

Ask God for God's unselfish and loving presence to enter into you. Also, ask for the grace to listen to what God has to say today.

Pray

Pray the passage from Scripture by reading it slowly aloud. Listen to the words, and then read them again. Pause at words or phrases that touch you. Cherish their beauty. Imagine God speaking them to you.

Close

Review your prayer. Think about what was most important in this prayer time. End with an Our Father. Record what happened in your prayer in the booklet.

Director's Guide

1 - Beginning to Pray

(Bring one light and one heavy hand weight. Place them near chair)

We all know that getting any benefit from exercise takes effort, determination, and repetition. Experts say aerobic exercise is important, and in order to not loose bone mass, strengthening exercises are vital too. But if I lift a heavy weight without training, I might pull a muscle and not gain benefit. To make any exercise program to work, I've got to start easy, with this smaller weight and add reps until I am strong enough to lift the heavy one. *(Point to weights or lift them as you speak)*

If we compare physical fitness to the ability to spiritual exercises, that is, communicating with God, we might recognize that spiritual exercises are similar to physical ones. When practice and repeat prayer, our spirit grows stronger. Like physical exercises, the process is slow and almost imperceptible and takes practice. It builds over time.

Physically, we may pull a muscle or rip a tendon if we move too quickly or don't follow the routine. This can happen spiritually also. Prayer is a process that opens us to vulnerable places within your soul – places of wounds, disillusionment, sorrow, and dysfunction. Bad habits, negative self-talk, wrong choices, rebellion, addictions, fear, and laziness all influence us negatively, and can slow our spiritual fitness. But here's the good part. You'll have a personal trainer to make sure you don't injure yourself by exercising in a harmful way. Your director guides your training such that your deepest joys, enthusiasms, love, power, and creativity work toward closer communion with God.

The Exercises have risks. You'll be exposed to deep and vulnerable places in your soul. But they also promise great rewards. Spiritual Exercising will bring you closer to God in new ways. If you allow the process to work, if you let God lead you, are willing to experience some "spiritual muscle burn," trial and error, and just plain hard work, you will indeed experience a spectacular event: communion with the God-self. We guarantee that you will come away from this experience transformed in some way.

For the retreat to be effective, it must be take high priority. Commit yourself to attending the weekly meetings, and praying daily. You'll grow stronger because of your commitment.

In a book called "Inviting the Mystic, supporting the Prophet, by Kathryn Dykman and Patrick Carroll, the authors describe prayer as essentially being in relationship with a living God who loves us, and who is, in fact obsessed with us. Prayer is Life. Prayer is gift and call.

In Isaiah 45:10 it says: "But my love for you will never leave you, even if mountains fall and hills turn to dust." In John 15:15 Jesus tells us, "I no longer call you servants but friends." Aren't these powerful images? There isn't a more intimate kind of relationship than one of husband and wife, or between friends. The Lord wants us to have that kind of relationship with God.

According to Jesus, I can find God within me. So I don't really have to journey out there somewhere. Rather, I journey into my heart. In our daily lives, every day, God calls each of us to journey even closer union. God loves us so much God wants us to explore our inner self.

Sometimes we actually believe that we can escape God. Perhaps we get the notion that God is some big parent or boss in the sky, waiting for us to ask what we should do, and most likely it will not be what we want. But that isn't the way God works. Instead, God wants to help each of us find out our truest self. God put our deepest desires there, so God has a vested interest in helping us achieve those desires.

The world tries all sorts of tactics to displace our deepest, God-centered desires with superficial ones. We can be lured to wealth, power, beauty, popularity, and vanity, all which prevent us from allowing growth or progression on our journey.

Prayer steers us away from the business of life and directs us into our inner world, where God resides. Prayer lets God get a word in edgewise. Prayer helps us become who we were meant from our creation to be.

Fr. Armand Negro S.J. says that prayer is something God does to us rather than anything we do. It's is our awareness of God within, and then our response to that presence. This awareness comes from us taking time to recognize God's constant longing to communicate with us.

How to Begin

Choose a passage from scripture. You'll be given Bible readings and other materials from which you can choose what to pray about each day. But this isn't a course. If a scripture speaks to you, stay with it for as many days as you like. Don't feel compelled to go on.

Find a place and time that works for you. Make it a place where you can be alone with God. I use my living room couch, but I know others who use their kitchen table, the dining room table, the family room, the patio, and the chapel. Try to find a spot where you will not be inhibited in responding to God as you pray, a place where you feel comfortable in all situations. Then use the same place every day… Make it a habitual time, and it will be easier.

The point of course, is not when we pray, but that we manage to do it. If you have trouble finding a time, ask God to carve out a time for you.

Choose a posture that is comfortable. At the beginning of your prayer time, settle yourself into a position that will be most conducive to prayer. Our body posture is important. Maybe you pray better kneeling, or standing with your hands outstretched, or laying flat on the floor. The prone position was one of Ignatius' favored positions. Experiment with various postures to see what works. I tried all sorts of positions, and found that most days, if I sit any other way than upright, I tend to doze.

Feel the presence of God. God is a God of the moment – "I am." So before you open your book or Bible, take a few minutes to enter into the moment. Feel your feet on the ground, your clothing against your skin, your breath going in and out of your lungs. See the colors of the room or the area, appreciate the moment, the now. Then acknowledge God's love for you. Thank God for loving you, for giving you all the gifts of your life, for self. Thank God for breath and life. Don't hurry. If this takes most of your prayer time, or even all of it, that's is OK.

Sometimes you'll feel God's presence, sometimes not. If you can't feel God, it doesn't mean God isn't present.

Pray the passage. Focus your prayer on listening to what God has to say rather than trying to put words into God's mouth. Get ready to God's love. But we can't make, steal, or earn it.

Close the session. Look back over your prayer in review. Consider what the Lord spoke to you and what you spoke to the Lord. Then pray the Our Father to end. When your prayer is finished, jot in your journal. Journaling is an important part of the experience. It helps you organize ideas and thoughts. For me, writing clarifies what I think or feel.

Summary

George Mahoney, S.J., in his book, Inward Stillness, wrote, "Prayer is not a mere conversation on words with God. It is more than striving to attain a nice, pleasant feeling. Ultimately it is a look upon God, a loving gaze that God the Holy Spirit infuses within us."

It's easy to let life sweep us into values and feelings. Yet, God desperately wants to communicate with us. To let this happen, we must slow down and be quiet. And, like physical exercise, this takes practice. Trust God. Seek God within your depths through the Exercises. Then be prepared for a powerful experience.

2 - The Life of Ignatius of Loyola

Through the Eyes of His Sister-in-Law

(This is very effective if presenter can dress in long brown robe and shawl and act this out.)

Hola! Me llamo Madalena de Araoz. I came from the 15th century Basque country of Spain to tell you about my brother-in-law, Inigo Lopez de Onaz y Loyola. He was the youngest son of eleven children – seven boys and four girls.

It's hard to know where to start the story. Before I was married, I worked at the palace where I was the Lady in waiting to Queen Isabella. There I heard about that amazing man, Christopher Columbus, who had just reached some new land with his fleet of three ships. That century had so much turmoil - full of revolution and discovery. In church, the priests warned us about Martin Luther and his cronies who threatened our holy mother the Church. Several people in the castle testified at the inquisitions. There was so much unrest and change.

My family was loyal to the Spanish Crown, of course, and we had honor, prestige, and jobs that mattered. But I get ahead of myself. Let me tell you more about my brother-in-law. Inigo was born in 1491. Sadly, his mother, my mother-in-law, died when Inigo was just two. Martin and I were newly married, but I felt sorry for baby Inigo and became his mother. After Inigo and Martin's father died, Martin, being the oldest, became heir to their family estate. Back then, it was common practice for youngest children to be dedicated to the church, so that is what we did with Inigo.

As Inigo grew, we realized that his personality was not suited to clerical life. He was a dandy, for sure. If we had known anything about the Enneagram, we would have said he was a four personality – a person of the heart who enjoys looking good. He wore his blond hair long and he dressed himself in colorful garb. As a teenager he served a family friend, the royal treasurer, Jan Velasquez de Cuellar, as a page. He told me many times that he hoped to prepare himself for the career of a courtier and soldier. That seemed to fit his personality well and he enjoyed the life of a young, single male courtier.

Inigo gambled, brawled, and fought in duels. He flirted and dallied with women and became a special admirer of the youngest daughter of Emperor Charles V. His friend, Velasquez got him a job in the court. But when Velasquez lost favor what the Spanish Monarch and was disgraced, dismissed, and finally died, Inigo was left master-less and disillusioned. I felt so badly for him. In those days, a person could hardly survive without a patron.

I tried to talk Inigo into staying and working for Martin, but he left in search of a lord to serve. He wrote us that he enlisted in the army of the Viceroy of Navarre and found himself defending Pamplona, the capital city of Navarre against a French army of 12,000 troops. Inigo convinced the commander not to surrender without a fight. In the ensuing battle, Inigo's right leg was shattered by a cannon ball and his left leg was badly injured.

After the fall of Pamplona, the French treated his wounds and arranged for Inigo to be carried home to Loyola. It took two torturous weeks for him to travel through the mountains. Upon his arrival in Loyola, of course I took him into our home again. We called the best doctors. To our dismay, they discovered that the bone had been poorly set and that even if it healed it would be shorter and a piece of the bone even protruded out of his leg. Inigo, proud man that he had become, was so concerned with looks that he demanded his bone be re-broken and set straight. The doctors did that, but it took a year of recovery. During the weeks that followed the re-break, he lingered dangerously near death. I felt frightened for him, watching him suffer, easing his fever, hearing his screams.

Eventually, though, Inigo began to improve. And just lying around in bed, he had a great deal of time on his hands. I remember him saying, "Madalena, bring me something to read that will entertain me – romance and chivalry."

"We don't have such books here in the castle," I told him. "All I have are the lives of Christ, of the saints, and the Bible." "I am so bored, I'll read anything," he said.

God certainly had a hand in Inigo's life, because gradually he changed. He told me that he paid attention to his fantasies and how they affected him. Even though he didn't know it at the time, this was the beginning of his rules for discernment. Whenever he fantasized about the glorious deeds he would do as a soldier he felt happy. But when the fantasies left him he felt let down and discontented. On the other hand, whenever he thought about the great deeds of the saints, like Dominic and Francis of Assisi, he felt exhilarated and full of energy. "Madelena," he said to me one day, "doing God's will is the only thing that will lead me to true peace. I must repent and be cleansed of my youthful sins!"

Once he recuperated, (though he still limped from the break, and one leg was shorter than the other) Inigo traveled to the famous monastery at Montserrat. It's about thirty miles from Barcelona, up a steep cliff. He rode a donkey up the winding trail to the monastery. There he stripped himself of his belongings, put on beggars' garb, and made a general confession. Then he spent the night in a vigil of prayer. The next morning he surrendered himself totally to God.

Without arms or money, a beggar really, Inigo headed back down the mountain to the small village of Manresa. He spent several months living at a Dominican monastery. He wrote me about the severe penances he inflicted on himself to make reparation for his sins. But I noticed a change in his mood. At first he had a great peace after his surrender to God at Montserrat. But that was replaced by tormenting scruples. He worried about all the sins he had committed, about the weight of those sins, and he seemed overwhelmed by it all. In some letters, Inigo actually despaired that God would never forgive him.

Director's Guide

At last the scruples left. He wrote to me, "My trial finally lifted when I humbly obeyed my director, who ordered me to break a prolonged, self-inflicted fast." I was so thankful that Inigo gradually allowed the comfort of God's grace into his soul. Slowly he was blessed with deep and consoling spiritual experiences.

There in Manresa, on the banks of the Cardoner River, God touched Inigo in a monumentally wonderful, deep, profound way. It was so profound that Inigo said it influenced him the rest of his life. He told me he learned more in that moment than he did in the whole rest of his life.

Ever since giving his life to God in Montserrat, Inigo had hoped to make a pilgrimage to the Holy Land. He talked of it often in his letters. And at last he felt ready to go. Without title, money, or possessions, he set out, begging as he went, for alms or food, and relying solely on the generosity of God.

As he made his way he wrote of his inner journey, describing his struggles with his desires for possessions and power. He also wrote of his own self-offering to God and his contemplations of the Incarnation, Christ's public life, passion, and resurrection. These meditative experiences became the foundation of his Spiritual Exercises.

Inigo needed the Pope's permission to go to Jerusalem, so he made his way to Rome and obtained permission for his pilgrimage. Just so you don't think that this man who devised the rules for discerning God's will always knew how to discern, I'd like to tell you this story. Inigo liked to tell it to keep himself humble and to highlight how important discernment really is. Inigo was traveling on a donkey down the road toward Rome when he met a Moor. The Moor stopped to talk, and insulted the Blessed Virgin. Inigo was incensed. After the Moor left, he headed off and went left at the fork of the road. Inigo could not decide if he should head left, follow the Moor, and kill him for the insult, or continue on his journey, to the right. He decided to let the donkey decide. Fortunately for all of us, Inigo's donkey took the right fork and the Moor lived another day.

To get to the Holy Land, Inigo begged for money and eventually did make it to Israel. There he excitedly visited all the holy places. After only three weeks the authorities asked him leave because they feared he would be killed or kidnapped like so many eager pilgrims before him. He left for Spain disappointed. Inigo told me that originally, he believed his mission was to convert unbelievers who lived in the Holy Land. So he planned to return some day. To tell you the truth, I was glad he came home. The Holy Land was a dangerous place, and I feared for his life.

On return to Spain, Inigo settled in Barcelona. There he decided to educate himself so that he could be a more effective preacher of God's word. He studied reading and writing with schoolboys. He told a story about the visions he had in school. He had been going to school for a while, and it was drudgery. Yet, because he knew he needed education, he persisted. Then, in the evenings, he started having wonderful visions of angels and Jesus. The visions lifted his ego and he felt special and holy. However, they lasted all evening, and at the end, he was so tired he could not study. Fortunately, he was smart enough to evaluate his life by then. He prayed about the visions, and asked God to remove them if they were a distraction and not from God. Amazingly, the visions disappeared and never returned. Inigo learned an important lesson about the evil spirit masquerading as the angel of light.

After two years, Inigo knew enough Latin to enter the University. He attended Alcala where he studied philosophy. At Alcala, Inigo lived in a poorhouse and made an income by giving instructions in the Spiritual Exercises. I worried so much about him. He suffered health problems that were the result of his earlier penances. Another stress he had came from frequent inquiries by the local church officials into the orthodoxy of his informal preaching and teaching. Eventually, Inigo was forbidden to teach until he had completed his studies.

Inigo and several companions who joined him moved to Salamanca where they hoped they might be better received. There also he was jailed on suspicion of heresy and forbidden to teach or preach. Inigo accepted that he must finish his studies for the priesthood and set off for Paris. There he studied philosophy and theology. At this time Inigo Latinized his name and began calling himself Ignatius. While in Paris he made the acquaintance of Peter Faber and Francis Xavier. They were both attracted by Ignatius' charm and by his ideals. More men joined them and eventually they formalized their commitment to follow Jesus by making vows of chastity, poverty, and promised to make a pilgrimage to Jerusalem.

The company of men later became known as the Society of Jesus. They took a special vow to the pope, and became the Pope's men. Ignatius and the pope sent Jesuits to teach and preach in many lands all over the world. One of the big disappointments in life for Ignatius was that his health never allowed him to return to the Holy Land. He wrote me several times wishing he could go there. He spent his last days administering the new religious order he had founded and guided both men and women, lay and religious, in the Spiritual Exercises.

These exercises are a rich legacy that Ignatius of Loyola has left the world. Many programs are based on the structure and content of the Exercises including the 12 step program for Alcoholics Anonymous. That is why I had to return to tell you about this great man. He wrote his exercises for lay people. He wanted to bring prayer and closeness to God to everyone.

I hope you enjoyed hearing about my brother-in-law who was really my little boy. I loved him dearly and see that when we dedicated his life to Christ while he was a baby, it really ended up that way. Inigo brought much to our world, and provided a light.

3 - Guided Meditation
The Saving Goodnes of Love

Read aloud. Pause at every "…" and where mentioned.

Sit quietly with your hands on your lap, feet flat against the floor. Just get comfortable…If you like, you can move to the floor. [Pause 15 seconds or so].

Breathe deeply in and out … Imagine your tension leaking from your feet like water through a hose. …Feel the tension drain from your feet upwards through your body … Notice how your stress drains down through your legs … Let anxiety and tension leave your stomach and chest … Now let it escape from your arms…and your shoulders … your neck … let your jaw and face relax…slow down…breathe in slowly, out slowly. [Pause 30 seconds]

Now imagine you are taking a stroll through a meadow toward the woods…see and feel yourself slowly walking along a winding path…tall grass and wildflowers wave in the soft, cool breeze … the sun caresses your face … you stop to take in the scene … [pause 30 seconds]

Birds flit among the wild flowers and fly into the pine trees ahead of you … Butterflies float among the flowers … One stops near you … You barely breathe so that it won't wing away … Now you inhale the fragrances carried on the wind … You breathe in and out deeply several times …[pause 30 seconds]

Slowly, you continue walking towards the woods… Up ahead, you notice a man sitting on a log in the shade … With a slight wave of his hand he greets you … You wave back …. When you get closer, he invites you to share the log with him…You sit down… You and the man sit together in silence for a moment or two, just appreciating the beauty all around you. [Pause 30 seconds]

When he says, "Peace be with you."...Your eyes are opened; you know that he is Jesus... Then Jesus reaches out and takes your hand. He looks deeply into your eyes and says, "I love you with an everlasting love...." [Pause 20 seconds]

"Now, my friend, let me show you the places in your life where you've encountered my love."

Your memory is filled now with people who have loved you, and people whom you have loved....Some come easily to your memory; others take more time, but Jesus helps you. [Pause for 3-5 minutes]

Jesus says, "Share stories of these people with me." You tell Jesus about a few of the beloved and loving people in your life...He listens carefully. [Pause again for 3-5 minutes]

Finally, Jesus stands to go. He says, "Blessed are you because you have loved so much." He embraces you. ...Then you watch as he walks slowly into the forest. ...

When he disappears, you gaze at the scene around you once more... the trees, the birds, the ferns, the log, the butterflies...

Then, when you are ready, you return from the scene to this room and open your eyes.

Amen.

(Adapted from Carl Koch, *Teaching Manual for Creating a Christian Lifestyle*, pp 99-100)

4 - Principle and Foundation

Note – bring two pictures: House being washed away by hurricane, whole home.

We usually take foundations for granted. Yet, almost all buildings have them. A foundation keeps a building from sinking, cracking, sliding, sagging, or blowing away. And they are specific for the building. The foundation matches exactly the building size. For instance, you can't have a 100x100 building perched on a 10x10 foundation. Spiritual foundations are similar to building foundations. A spiritual foundation is important. We need one to grow spiritually. As with buildings, a spiritual foundation keeps us from loosing our spiritual balance, sinking into mud of sin, or even washing away. *(Show house in hurricane picture)*

To build a spiritual mansion, you've got to start with the right sized foundation, and one strong enough to support the weight. Fortunately for us, Ignatius helps us with both these issues. His Principle and Foundation pours concrete concept slabs on which we can attach the joists of our spiritual growth. These concrete principles allow us to begin building additions to our faith life.

History of the Principle and Foundation

At Cardoner, Ignatius experienced God in a way that, he said, taught him more than he learned in all the rest of his life experiences put together. God revealed to him how God is the origin of all things, at all times. At all times God radiates the divine life, knowledge, and love, so that everything lives and moves in God. Ignatius also "saw" how Jesus came into our flesh, giving greater-than-human importance to human desires and emotions. He assumes we already love God, have accepted Jesus as savior, and want to follow God.

From that experience, Ignatius developed the *Principle and Foundation*. I'd like to read this to you now. I've put his words into first person for easier understanding during this talk.
[23] *I am created to praise, reverence, and serve God our Lord, and by this means, to save my soul. The other things on the face of the earth*

are created to help me attain the end for which I am created. Hence, I should make use of them as far as they help me in the attainment of my end, and must rid myself of them in as far as they prove a hindrance to me.

Therefore, I must make myself indifferent to all created things, as far as I am allowed by free choice and are not under any prohibition. As far as I am concerned, I should not prefer health to sickness, riches to poverty honor to dishonor a long life to a short life. The same holds true for all other things. My one desire and choice should be what is more conducive to the end for which I am created.

Creation Theology is important to our foundation. God is the author of all things, so all living things grow through phases and stages throughout life because of God. This is God's creation. Astronomy shows that stars are constantly being formed. The sun produces new elements through the atomic process going on within it. This too, is God creating. Closer to our own lives, babies are born, grow and change. Food we eat turns into us; we grow older. Our spirits grows closer or further from God each moment. God keeps creating, moment by moment.

Ignatius continues, *So I am to live among created things, focusing on certain ones, or not, setting aside some, picking up others, depending on whether they help me grow closer to God."* So how can I know what I should prefer?

Desires

Our goal in all this is to become more Christ-like. But doing that is complex. How can I begin? Somehow I must sift through everything God has put on this Earth to find what bring me closer to God, and which take me further away.

We might begin with asking "What would Jesus do?" It's a good start. But how can we know what Jesus would do in our situation? Looking again at the Principle and Foundation, I see that Ignatius says that I must make myself *"indifferent"* to all created things.

Indifference (or passion, its opposite) is how attached I am to something. To be consciously indifferent, I have to first know what I am attracted to. I must pay attention to my desires. I have to look at what I want deeply, and say to myself, "Yes, I want that, or even crave. This takes introspection and God's help.

Indifference

Then, we must ask ourselves, "What does God call me to?" And finally, "Am I willing to set that aside if God calls me to do so?" To be indifferent means I make a choice about whatever life presents me: choose a career, a place to live, to have a child or not, to marry or not, to work at a certain job, to volunteer for a specific activity-- not because our culture says it is great, not because others believe it's right for me, not because it is common belief, or my parents, friends, or a TV ad says it is right. Rather, when choices appear, to be indifferent, I'm open to choosing God's way, whatever that is.

Making a Choice Based on God

This might mean I opt for a lesser-paying job to serve in a place I feel called. It might mean I choose obscurity over the limelight or even the limelight over obscurity because I feel called there by God. Or I choose some position that provides less health care because God wants me there. Avoiding (or even seeking) poverty, obscurity, or long life cannot be the main deciding factors of a decision. To follow God completely, I've got to accept the basic foundational principle of Ignatius that in relation to my desires. Nothing, no desire of mine, compares in importance to pleasing God and enacting the desires he creates in the depths of my self.

Let me give you an example. When my youngest daughter went to school, I finally had time to do some of the things I always wanted. I started writing and joined a Bible study. Then problems arose. Because of her visual impairment, kids made fun of her. She went into deep depression and finally, she wouldn't go to school at all. I kept her home for a week, trying to decide what to do. With more prayer, discussion with the psychologist, my husband, and the teacher, we decided that she needed to stay home for an extended period. So I began home schooling.

But I had to work hard to counteract my own desires – the Bible study and such. I gave up freedom and doing "good deeds" to follow what I knew was the right path. I went against traditional society, the establishment, peers and relatives who told me I was crazy. It wasn't easy, but it was a decision that has proved to be absolutely the best possible thing I could have done for her. *(Give your own example.)*

Attachments

Too easily we can get attached to lesser desires—the "false gods" of our world. And there are many of these. I'll list just a few.

1) Deadly Attachments are in the news every day. These include addictions of every type – alcohol, money, shopping, exercise, drugs, sex, etc, because they chain people to created things and prevent the captive from finding God within.

2) Serious attachments happen when we let our lives revolve around pleasures such as food, sports, work, television, or the Internet, blind us to what we are called to.

For example, I used to be overly focused on sugar. I hovered around snack tables to make sure I got to try all the goodies. Through prayer and discernment, I realized how attached I was. I knew I had to stop eating sugar. For two years I rationalized all sorts of reasons why it would be too hard. Then, with God's help, I finally quit eating it, and it has freed me. (Give your own example.)

3) Even small attachments can hinder our commitment to follow God. People can grow overly focused on work, the internet, shopping, eating, coffee, control – almost anything, actually.

For those who love and want to follow God, it's important to give all decisions, even "good" or insignificant ones, to God. How do I balance exercise, prayer, relationships and service? Faced with any good thing or interesting opportunity, if I love God, I must weigh what leads to deeper love, and what brings me to my truer self.

Prohibition

Some decisions have major consequences. Ignatius calls it "prohibition." What this means is that once I have made a decision that involves a solemn promise, I am no longer free in that area. For instance, I have chosen to marry so I'm not free to reconsider that decision. As Ignatius says, I am "under prohibition."

Summary

In Summary, the Principle and Foundation says I believe that I am constantly being created and that God will direct me to his will for me. When I face a serious choice, I will try not to have made up my mind ahead of time before I know or consider the alternatives. I wait for my choices to present themselves. I try not to favor one over another until I know clearly that God is speaking through my desires, or those of the Church, or others. I'm even willing to stand against culture if called to do so. I choose not to prefer something just because everyone else does. I equally consider wealth, poverty, fame, insignificance, good or lousy job, education or ignorance, notoriety or unimportance, good or poor health, long or short life. Every option is of equal value until I know clearly what God calls me to in this specific instance. Not till then do I act. I realize that I am "under prohibition" for some choices. And I accept the fact that some prior choices preclude future ones.

The Principle and Foundation challenges us to focus on what we believe, on what we will base our decisions. It will allow you broader, more solid spiritual construction because it can withstand the worst spiritual storms, floods, winds and quakes. What kind of foundation have you built? Is it the right size and strength to hold your mansion?

Show the whole, good-looking house picture.

Director's Guide

5 - Choosing the Exercises

Last January I signed up at a local gym for a ten-week program of exercises to see if I liked the place. I promised to attend three classes a week. At the end of the time, they asked me if I wanted to continue. I didn't have the time, so I turned down the offer.

This is where you are in relationship to the Spiritual Exercises. You have to decide whether to continue or not. And as you sift through your needs, values, ideas, hopes, and dreams, and what you think God is calling you to, you get the opportunity to practice discernment. It isn't easy.

While praying through the Preparation Days Retreat, you've learned more than you think. You know that this is not a class or a seminar. Rather, it's not about developing a relationship with God through prayer; it's about experiencing and testing and listening deeply. They are what they are called – Exercises. They are more like a workout session with a personal trainer than a class on the physiology. Thus, they require that a person work through them. This means retreatants commit to daily personal prayer time (an hour is best), meet with their assigned director, and practice listening to what's happening within. The Exercises are a personal journey toward spiritual strength, based on an individual's spiritual fitness level. We even provide a personal trainer to help people through.

During the past weeks, you've been presented with principles that are foundational to the Exercises. St. Ignatius learned from God, at the River Cardoner, more than he learned in all the rest of his life experiences put together, all about how God is the origin of all things, at all times. He wrote how at all times God radiates the divine life, knowledge, and love, so that everything lives and moves in God. Ignatius also "saw" how Jesus came into our flesh, giving greater-than-human importance to human desires and emotions. But none of this was a new revelation to Ignatius. The Bible tells us all this also. He just reformatted it for easy understanding. And

Ignatius thought it so important and foundational that he called it the *Principle and Foundation*. You heard it last week. It says:

[23] *I am created to praise, reverence, and serve God our Lord, and by this means, to save my soul. The other things on Earth are created to help me attain the end for which I am created. Hence, I should make use of them as far as they help me in the attainment of my end, and must rid myself of them in as far as they prove a hindrance to me.*

Therefore, I must make myself indifferent to all created things, as far as I am allowed by free choice and are not under any prohibition. As far as I am concerned, I should not prefer health to sickness, riches to poverty honor to dishonor a long life to a short life. The same holds true for all other things. My one desire and choice should be what is more conducive to the end for which I am created.

How can I know what God wants me to focus on, what helps me become more Christ-like? The answer, of course, is discernment – figuring out God's will for my life. And during this retreat, you will learn those rules and have the opportunity to practice them.

Desires

God has put on this Earth at my disposal, but to do God's will, we have to sort through all of it and choose what it is that will bring us closer to God. This sorting is discernment.

God doesn't want us to follow him as much as he wants us to be close enough to God to trust him. I sift things so I can find what bring me closer to God, and which things take me further away.

We might begin with asking "What would Jesus do?" It's a good start. But how can we know what Jesus would do in our situation? Looking again at the Principle and Foundation, I see that Ignatius says that I must make myself *"indifferent"* to all created things. Indifference (or passion, its opposite) is how attached I am to something. To be consciously indifferent, I have to first know what I am attracted to. I must pay attention to my desires. I have to look at what I want deeply, and say to myself, "Yes, I want that, or even crave. This takes introspection and God's help.

Indifference

The Principle and Foundation also talks about indifference. This isn't a common understanding of the word – I don't care. Rather, it means I'm not overly focused on any particular outcome other than doing God's will. Then, we must ask ourselves, "What does God call me to?" And finally, "Am I willing to set that aside if God calls me to do so?" To be indifferent means I make a choice about whatever life presents me: choose a career, a place to live, to have a child or not, to marry or not, to work at a certain job, to volunteer for a specific activity-- not because our culture says it is great, not because others believe it's right for me, not because it is common belief, or my parents, friends, or a TV ad says it is right. Rather, when choices appear, to be indifferent, I'm open to choosing God's way, whatever that is.

Making a Choice Based on God

The group meetings for the Exercises will be the first Saturday of every month beginning (Date) _____ and continuing through (Date) _____. Some of the questions you can ask yourself in making this decision include:

1. Am I willing to pray for ½ to one hour per day, even if that means I let go of something I enjoy, such as television or a social activity or even another spiritual activity?
2. Do I commit to attend the monthly group meetings?
3. Am I willing to journal about my prayer experiences?
4. Will I be faithful in meeting with my director? Am I willing to share my spiritual experiences with him or her?
5. Will my family be supportive of my intention to participate in the Spiritual Exercises?
    6. What desires has God placed in my heart at this time? What do I think God has to say about this?
    7. What reservations do I have?

I want to trust that I am constantly being created and God will direct me to his will for me. But to do so, I have to know God well enough to trust.

When I face a serious choice, I want to wait for my choices to present themselves and not run ahead of God, not favor one over another until I know clearly that God is speaking through my desires, or those of the Church, or others. Sometimes, I'm even willing to stand against culture if I think God is calling me to it. Only until I choose God first can I do this. Only with deep prayer, understanding the things that drive me, listening carefully to the quiet voice within me, can I begin to sift through it all and see what God calls me to in each specific instance.

This is what the Exercises can do for you – teach you how to listen, to truly know God. This is what the Exercises are meant to do – change your heart and help you know who you truly are. If you are ready for this journey, we invite you to join us. It will be a ride of a lifetime, a spectacular workout.

Questions for contemplation:
What desires has God placed in my heart about the Exercises?
What reservations do I have?
Where am I called to be?

Director's Guide

Sample Brochure

Please see the following four pages for a sample brochure.

You can receive a FREE digital copy of this file in MS Word to add your own contact information.

Just send an e-mail to Ellen at spiritualexercises@msn.com and ask for the Prep Days Retreat file.

"Come away with me to a quiet place"

You're invited

Preparation Days

Retreat

Five Weeks of Ignatian Prayer

Application for Preparation Days Retreat

Your answers will be kept confidential.

NAME_____PHONE_____

ADDRESS _____

CITY/STATE_____ ZIP_____

E-MAIL_____ CELL_____

I learned about Spiritual Exercises from:

1. How do you see God?

    2. How would you like to know God?

    3. What do you hope to gain from this retreat?

    4. What experiences (if any) have you had with spiritual direction? (This can include a prayer partner, a directed retreat, or direction)?

I'm willing to commit to daily personal prayer _____
I'm willing to commit to the 5 weekly meetings _____
(If you can't make any particular meeting, we'd like to know ahead of time.)

Cost is by donation. We ask $_____ which helps cover all materials as well as training for our directors, but it's up to you. You can pay ahead or at the door.

___ $__ enclosed. I'll pay at the door___ I'll donate other $____
Make checks payable to: _____ Mail application to:

About the Preparation Days Retreat

God is alive today and desires to speak to each one of us. Yet, many of us don't know how to listen for God's voice. The Preparation Days Retreat, the first part of the Spiritual Exercises, provides a way in which you can develop your prayer life and learn how to better listen to God.

During this retreat you will have the opportunity to:
- Practice meditative prayer using scripture
- Practice small group spiritual direction
- Pray about how much God loves you
- Develop a personal spiritual foundation
- Learn more about St. Ignatius and the spirituality he developed, and how it fits into your life.
- Prepare for the Spiritual Exercises (if you choose to continue)

We invite you to join the Preparation Days Retreat. Taste and see how good prayer can be for you.

Preparation Days Retreat Details

Time and Dates
Place
Cost
All materials will be provided

When you complete the Preparation Days Retreat, you will be given the opportunity to continue into the full Spiritual Exercises in Everyday Life Retreat. You'll receive more information during the Preparation Days Retreat, and you'll be given the opportunity to pray about and discern whether continuing is right for you. If you choose to continue, you will be asked to hand in your faith autobiography, which you will write during the Preparation Days Retreat. For more on the Exercises see the back of this brochure or contact:

About The Spiritual Exercises

The Spiritual Exercises present participants with a deep and powerful prayer experience. During this retreat, through practice, you'll learn contemplation, meditation and other forms of prayer. You'll be taught and given a chance to practice the rules for discernment, while growing in faith, hope, and love. Most importantly, you'll develop a deeper relationship with God. We guarantee that if you complete this retreat, your life will be changed in wonderful ways.

If you choose to continue into the Exercises, we'll ask you to commit to:
- Attend monthly group meetings, November - May
- Meet at least once every two weeks with your assigned spiritual director (on your own schedule)
- Pray for one hour daily using materials we provide (on your own schedule)
- Keep a prayer journal

The cost of the Exercises is $____ per month, November through May for a total of $____ for the whole retreat.

About Your Retreat Team

Write something about your team, and their expertise, and how many people you have.

Meeting Schedule Overview

	Date	Subject	Presenter	MC / Enviro	Prayer	Snack
1		How to Pray				
2		Ignatius Story & sharing				
3		Guided meditation				
4		Principle & Foundation				
5		Faith autobiog. & Continue the Exercises				

List the names of the persons responsible for each task in each block.

Director's Guide

NOTES:

www.ingramcontent.com/pod-product-compliance
Lightning Source LLC
Chambersburg PA
CBHW071758040426
42446CB00012B/2607